Contents

Watery world

Earth is a blue planet. Around 70 per cent of its surface is covered in water. Most is found in its five huge oceans, but there are also smaller pockets of water found in seas, lakes and rivers. Within these watery worlds is a huge range of habitats that are home to an even bigger range of living things.

Coastal habitats
Where the sea meets land can be a brutal place to live, as waves pound the shore and the tides pull the water in and out.

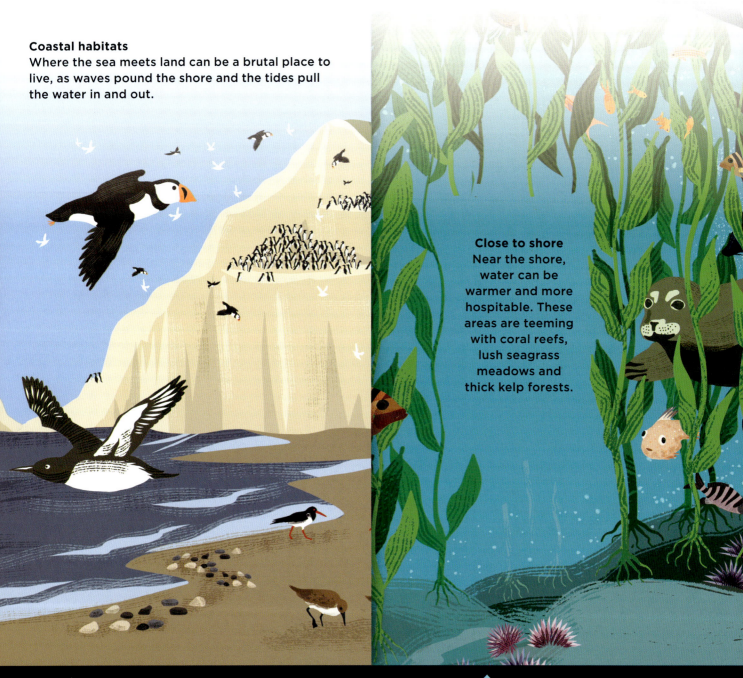

Close to shore
Near the shore, water can be warmer and more hospitable. These areas are teeming with coral reefs, lush seagrass meadows and thick kelp forests.

STARTING WITH THE BIGGEST, THE FIVE OCEANS ARE:

Pacific Ocean 168,723,000 square km

Atlantic Ocean 85,133,000 square km

Indian Ocean 70,560,000 square km

Southern Ocean 21,960,000 square km

Arctic Ocean 15,558,000 square km

Out at sea
Far from land, the vast open ocean has a small number of living things scattered over a huge area.

Deep dark place
Far below the surface, the oceans are dark and cold. No light reaches below a depth of 1,000 m and the weight of the water exerts crushing pressure. Even so, many living things make the deep ocean their home.

Under threat
Global warming is seeing a steady rise in sea levels as polar ice melts into the oceans and warmer waters expand, threatening low-lying habitats. Pollution also dumps huge amounts of waste into the oceans. Floating plastics form enormous islands of rubbish, or break down into tiny particles that can be eaten by fish and enter the food chain.

THE OCEANS HOLD ABOUT **96.5%** OF ALL OF EARTH'S WATER.

THAT'S EQUIVALENT TO **1,338,000,000** CUBIC KM OF WATER.

Up to **12.7 million tonnes of plastic** enters the oceans every year.

River mouths

OPENING TO THE SEA

Africa's mighty River Nile flows into the Mediterranean Sea through the Nile Delta in Egypt. The delta is flat and fertile. The land here has been used for farming for thousands of years.

Forming a fan
As the Nile approaches the sea, it slows down, and starts to drop a fine material called sediment. This builds up, dividing the river into smaller channels that spread out into a fan shape.

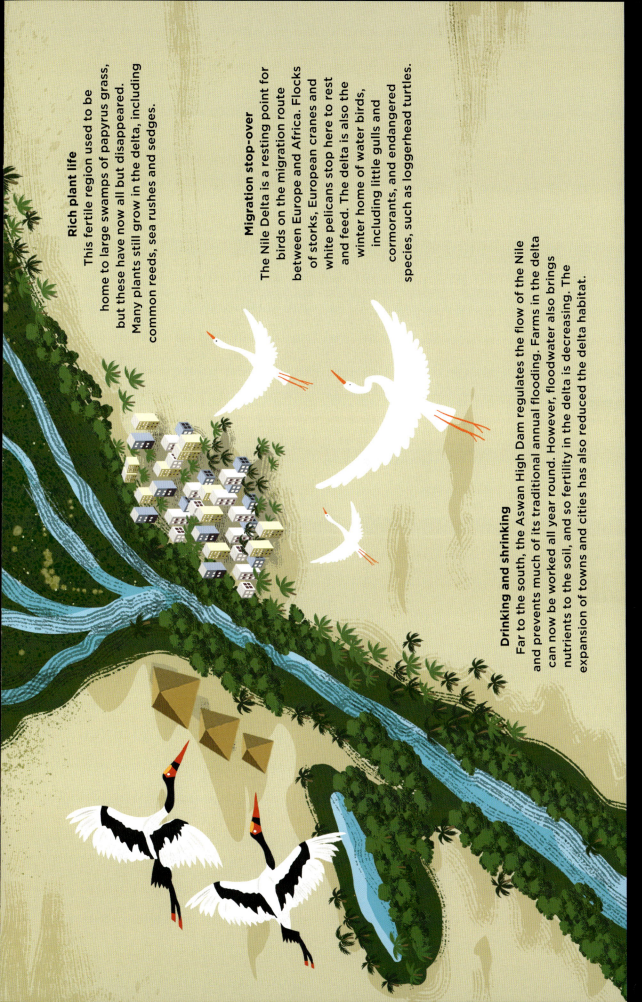

Rich plant life

This fertile region used to be home to large swamps of papyrus grass, but these have now all but disappeared. Many plants still grow in the delta, including common reeds, sea rushes and sedges.

Migration stop-over

The Nile Delta is a resting point for birds on the migration route between Europe and Africa. Flocks of storks, European cranes and white pelicans stop here to rest and feed. The delta is also the winter home of water birds, including little gulls and cormorants, and endangered species, such as loggerhead turtles.

Drinking and shrinking

Far to the south, the Aswan High Dam regulates the flow of the Nile and prevents much of its traditional annual flooding. Farms in the delta can now be worked all year round. However, floodwater also brings nutrients to the soil, and so fertility in the delta is decreasing. The expansion of towns and cities has also reduced the delta habitat.

The term **'delta'** comes from the Greek letter of the same name, which is written using a triangle.

THE NILE DELTA IS **175 KM LONG** AND **260 KM WIDE,** COVERING AN AREA OF **26,000 SQUARE KM.**

The Nile itself is **6,695 km long** and has a river basin that covers **3,026,000 square km.**

The Nile Delta is full of wildlife, including turtles, mongooses and the Nile monitor lizard.

7

Coasts

WHERE LAND MEETS SEA

Coastal habitats range from sheer cliffs to broad mudflats. The animals living on the shoreline have to adapt to survive ever-changing conditions as seawater rises and falls with the tides.

Cliffs and caves

The power of waves as they slam into rocky coasts carves out distinct features, including towering cliffs, caves, sea stacks and arches. These provide a safe home for seabirds, such as puffins and guillemots.

Beach life

As waves carve out rocky features, the debris is pounded down into pebbles or sand. This is carried away by the sea and dropped in calmer areas to form beaches. Sand provides shelter for invertebrates such as lugworms and razor clams, which burrow into it for safety when the tide goes out.

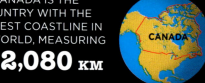

CANADA IS THE COUNTRY WITH THE LONGEST COASTLINE IN THE WORLD, MEASURING

202,080 KM

CANADA

IN COMPARISON, THE PRINCIPALITY OF MONACO HAS A COASTLINE THAT MEASURES ONLY

4 KM.

Threats
Coastal ecosystems are threatened by the spread of settlements and industry. Pollution has a major impact on these habitats. Sewage and chemicals poison wildlife, while rubbish can trap and harm animals.

Mudflat food web
Formed by sediments dropped by rivers, coastal mudflats are rich in nutrients that feed tiny microbes. The microbes are food for burrowing worms and molluscs, which attract seabirds, such as oystercatchers, who pluck food out of the mud using their long bills.

The white cliffs of Dover are made from the skeletons of tiny living things called coccoliths. These built up on top of each other over millions of years when the area was covered by the sea.

A SINGLE SQUARE METRE OF SANDY BEACH CAN BE HOME TO 20,000 BURIED LUGWORMS.

Between the tides

A CHANGING HABITAT

When the tide is high, seawater covers the coastline, but at low tide small pools of water are left behind in the cracks and spaces between rocks. Living inside these pools is a wide range of creatures, from tiny invertebrates to fish.

Exposed rocks
The area of coast that is covered with water at high tide and exposed at low tide is called the intertidal zone. When the water retreats, anything living here has to cope with direct sunlight and pounding waves. Barnacles and limpets grip firmly to the exposed rocks, waiting for the water to return.

High tide zone
Closer to the sea, rock pools are left by the retreating tide and are home to seaweed and an array of creatures, such as colourful anemones, mussels and crabs.

Low tide zone
This part of the shoreline remains underwater most of the time. A greater range of living things can survive here, including small fish, such as blennies, gobies and pipefish.

Rock pool hunters
Trapped in the rock pool, creatures are vulnerable to predators. Starfish will crawl onto mussels, pull their shells apart and then extend their stomachs out through their mouths to eat the shellfish! Hungry gulls snatch up urchins and drop them to break their shells open to eat.

The rise and fall of the tides is caused by the gravitational pull of the Moon and the Sun.

TIDES AT THE BAY OF FUNDY IN CANADA HAVE A RANGE OF 15 M, THE GREATEST IN THE WORLD.

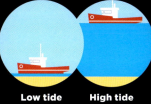

Low tide   **High tide**

The material that makes up limpets' teeth is the strongest known natural substance. The limpets use their teeth to scrape food such as algae off solid rock.

HERMIT CRABS DO NOT GROW THEIR OWN SHELL. INSTEAD, THEY USE THE EMPTY SHELLS OF OTHER ANIMALS, SUCH AS WHELKS OR SNAILS. AS THEY GROW, THEY MOVE TO LARGER SHELLS.

Mangroves

SALTY HABITATS

Mangrove forests grow along tropical coastlines where the tide floods over the land twice a day, creating a salty habitat where only a few plants can survive.

Special roots
Mangroves are trees that have adapted to living in very salty water. They stand on stilt roots that keep most of the tree above the water line, even at high tide. Their wide roots have special holes in them through which the tree takes in the gases they need to survive.

Snorkel roots
Some mangroves grow slim pencil-like breathing roots that stick up out of the water. Called pneumatophores, they allow the trees to take in air from above the water.

Threatened mangroves
Mangrove forests are being cleared to make way for coastal cities and shrimp farms. Rising sea levels caused by global warming also threaten to submerge many mangrove forests completely.

Safe haven
Mangrove roots provide a safe home for invertebrates, such as brittle stars and sea urchins. They are also a great place for small fish to hide and breed. Larger fish, such as small sharks, are attracted to the mangrove forests by the rich prey.

MANGROVES LIVE IN WATER THAT'S **100 TIMES SALTIER** THAN MOST OTHER PLANTS CAN TOLERATE. THEIR ROOTS FILTER OUT THE SALT AND SOME SPECIES CAN EXCRETE IT THROUGH THEIR LEAVES.

35% OF THE WORLD'S MANGROVES HAVE ALREADY DISAPPEARED, AND IN MANY COUNTRIES, IT IS **AS HIGH AS 50%.**

Mangrove forests help to protect land during a hurricane. They act as a buffer, absorbing much of a storm surge before it can do much damage.

13

Seagrass meadows

UNDERWATER PASTURES

Just like grasslands on land, these underwater meadows provide a home for both small animals and large grazers and can be found in nearly all of the seas and oceans, from the Arctic Circle to the tropics.

Underwater plants
Seagrasses have leaves, roots and veins, just like grasses on land. They also produce flowers and seeds. Like plants on land, seagrasses make their own food using sunlight and carbon dioxide gas.

Smaller creatures
Seagrass provides good cover for tiny micro-organisms, like algae. These attract larger living things to feed, including crabs, sea urchins and fish. Just one hectare of seagrass can be home to 80,000 fish and 100 million small invertebrates.

Underwater grazers
Seagrass grazers include green sea turtles and large mammals called dugongs. In one day, a fully grown dugong can munch up to 40 kg of seagrass.

Going, going...
Seagrass meadows are being lost at a rate of two football pitches every hour. They are being destroyed by pollution, damage from boat propellers and rising sea temperatures.

SEAGRASSES GROW IN SALTY OR SEMI-SALTY (BRAKISH) WATERS AROUND THE WORLD, USUALLY CLOSE TO A COASTLINE.

IN REALLY CLEAR WATER, WHERE LIGHT CAN TRAVEL DEEPER, SEAGRASS MEADOWS CAN GROW AT DEPTHS OF ALMOST

60 M.

72
THE NUMBER OF KNOWN SEAGRASS SPECIES GROWING AROUND THE WORLD.

Seagrass meadows cover just 1 per cent of the sea floor, but are responsible for around 11 per cent of the carbon dioxide captured by the ocean.

Coral reef

TEEMING WITH LIFE

Tropical coral reefs are one of the richest habitats on Earth, supporting thousands of animal and plant species. They are found in warm ocean waters close to the equator.

Tiny builders

Coral reefs are built by small creatures called polyps. These provide a home for tiny algae, which pass nutrients to the polyps in return. The algae give the coral its vibrant range of colours. Coral polyps cover themselves with a tough outer shell. Over time, these shells build up to form a reef.

Types of reef

There are many different types of coral reef. The main ones are:

Fringing reef – a reef directly attached to the shore.

Barrier reef – a reef separated from the shore by a lagoon or water channel.

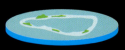

Atoll – a ring-shaped reef with a lagoon in the middle.

Wildlife paradise
With lots of nooks and crannies to hide in, and plenty of food available, coral reefs support a varied and vibrant ecosystem. Reef species range from clams and sponges to seahorses, turtles and sharks.

Under attack
Crown-of-thorns starfish can eat so much coral that their numbers are sometimes controlled. Other threats to reefs include pollution, tourism and dynamite fishing. Most damaging of all, however, are rising sea temperatures, which can cause the coral to expel the algae. This is known as coral bleaching and turns healthy reefs into ghostly skeletons.

THE **GREAT BARRIER REEF** IS THE WORLD'S LARGEST CORAL REEF AND STRETCHES FOR ABOUT **2,300 KM** ALONG AUSTRALIA'S NORTHWEST COAST.

Great
Barrier Reef

AUSTRALIA

Even though coral reefs make up just **0.1 per cent** of the oceans' area, they are home to about **25 per cent** of all ocean species.

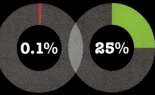

0.1%   25%

THERE ARE MORE THAN 25,000 SPECIES OF CORAL.

Kelp forest

TOWERING ALGAE

These thick coastal forests create a dense habitat that provides a perfect home for grazing shellfish, sea otters, fish and seals. Kelp forests exist in shallow waters around the world.

Plants?

They may look like tall trees, but kelps aren't plants at all. Instead, they are large brown algae. A single kelp forest can contain many different species of kelp.

Holding fast

The kelp is attached to the seabed by a root-like structure called a holdfast. Growing out of this is the stipe, which is like a plant's stem. Long, leafy fronds are attached to the stipe, alongside small gas-filled bladders that keep the kelp afloat.

Safe shelter
The kelp provides an ideal home for many species. Fish such as lumpsuckers lay their eggs here, while mammals including sea otters, sea lions and even grey whales shelter and feed among the dense kelp fronds.

Greedy urchins
Sea urchins can nibble though the base of the kelp at a rate of about 9 m a month, which can clear an entire kelp forest. Other threats include pollution, warming of the seas and overfishing, which can allow sea urchin numbers to grow unchecked.

In the right conditions, kelp can grow up to 60 cm in a single day!
That's about the height of a medium-sized dog!

SOME SPECIES OF KELP CAN GROW TO MORE THAN 45 M LONG.

Kelp forests usually grow in cold, nutrient-rich waters where the algae can use sunlight to photosynthesise.

Sea otters protect the kelp forest environment by eating sea urchins.

Open ocean

ENORMOUS ECOSYSTEM

Great expanses of the world's seas and oceans lie far from land. Although this ocean realm is a huge habitat, it is largely empty. But the presence of a food source, such as a shoal of fish, can attract many visitors.

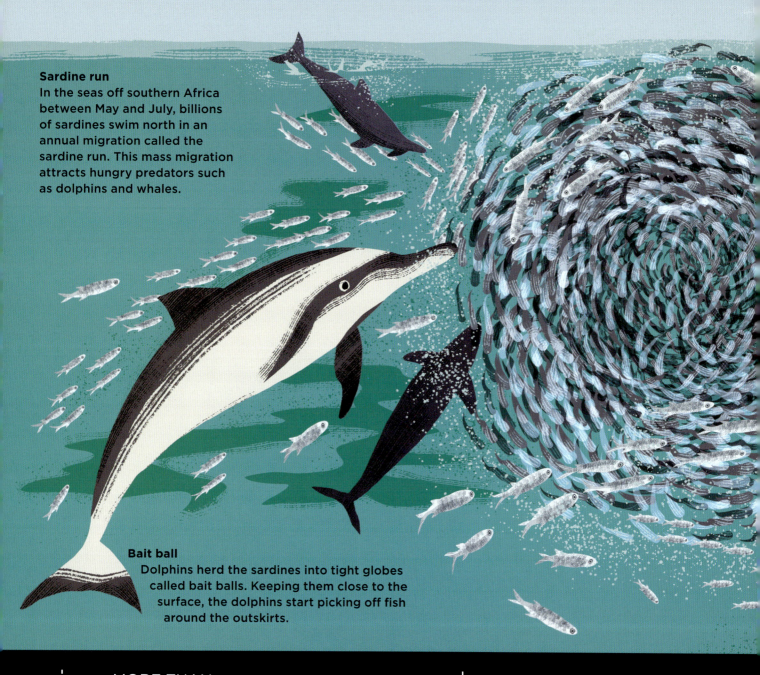

Sardine run
In the seas off southern Africa between May and July, billions of sardines swim north in an annual migration called the sardine run. This mass migration attracts hungry predators such as dolphins and whales.

Bait ball
Dolphins herd the sardines into tight globes called bait balls. Keeping them close to the surface, the dolphins start picking off fish around the outskirts.

MORE THAN

50%

OF EARTH'S SURFACE IS COVERED BY OCEAN THAT IS MORE THAN **3.2 KM DEEP.**

THE **GREAT PACIFIC GARBAGE PATCH** IS THE LARGEST ACCUMULATION OF PLASTIC POLLUTION IN THE OPEN OCEAN, STRETCHING **1.6 MILLION SQUARE KM.**

Attack from above

Above the surface, seabirds, such as gannets and cormorants, dive bomb the bait ball, plunging into the water to snatch up whatever fish they can.

Smash and grab

Other predators, including tuna and sharks, take advantage of all this prey, charging in to gobble up fish.

Plastic pollution

The open ocean is still affected by humans. Huge, swirling ocean currents sweep up waste from near the shore, creating floating islands of rubbish that can kill ocean wildlife that swallow or become entangled in discarded plastic and nets.

THE OPEN OCEAN IS KNOWN AS THE PELAGIC ZONE. IT INCLUDES ALL THE OCEANS, EXCEPT FOR COASTAL WATERS AND THE SEA FLOOR.

Pelagic zone

ONLY
10%
OF OCEAN SPECIES LIVE IN THIS ENORMOUS HABITAT.

21

Ocean deep

DARK AND CRUSHING

Deep below the surface, the water is inky black and mostly empty of life. Anything that does live down here has to deal with enormous water pressure and living in the constant dark.

Crushing pressures

At the deepest part of the ocean, pressures are about 1,100 times greater than at the surface. Deep-sea fish contain lots of water, which cannot be squashed, so they keep their shape under extreme pressure.

Lack of light

Very little sunlight reaches 200 m below the water's surface, and the water below 1,000 m is completely black. Animals living at these depths have adapted to live in the dark. Some have huge eyes or eyes on stalks to collect what little light there is.

Making light

Some living things can make their own light. Lantern fish have light organs beneath their eyes, which act like headlights. Anglerfish use a lure on the tops of their heads to attract prey.

Feeding ground

Food is very scarce. Most arrives when the dead body of a large fish or whale sinks to the sea floor. Hagfish burrow into the body, while scavenger sharks and crabs pick the bones clean. The Osedax worm grows 'roots' into the bones to feed on the rich marrow inside.

When threatened, deep-sea green bomber worms release small glowing bombs to confuse predators.

The Mariana Trench in the Pacific is the deepest part of the ocean. It lies

10,994 m

beneath sea level.

99%

OF THE OCEAN FLOOR IS UNEXPLORED.

Many creatures that live in the deepest parts of the ocean are actually **TRANSPARENT.**

Hydrothermal vents
LIVING AT THE EXTREME

Deep below the ocean's surface, scientists have discovered a unique ecosystem – one that doesn't need the energy of the Sun to support its living things.

Underwater fountains
Hydrothermal vents form when seawater seeps down through tiny cracks in the sea floor. Beneath the surface, the water is heated by molten rock and then shoots back out of the vents as hot plumes of water.

Underwater towers
As the hot water gushes out of the vents it reacts with the cold seawater, causing it to deposit sulphur and other minerals it was carrying. These build up to form tall towers.

Rich in minerals
Unlike creatures on land or near the water's surface, the tiny microbes that live around these vents don't need sunlight to feed themselves. Instead, they use the minerals in the hot water to make energy.

Unique food chain
The microbes form the basis of a deep-sea food chain. The energy they produce is passed onto many other living things as they are eaten, including tube worms, shrimp and mussels.

WATER GUSHING OUT OF THE VENTS CAN REACH TEMPERATURES OF **400°C – HOT ENOUGH TO MELT LEAD.**

- -

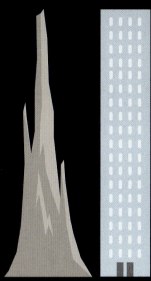

THESE TOWERS OF MINERALS CAN MEASURE UP TO 55 M TALL – AS HIGH AS AN 18 STOREY BUILDING.

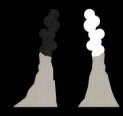

'Black smokers' are hydrothermal vents that are formed from iron sulphide.

'White smokers' are hydrothermal vents that are formed from barium, calcium and silicon.

- -

HYDROTHERMAL VENTS WERE ONLY DISCOVERED IN 1977.

Arctic waters
THE FROZEN NORTH

Covering the North Pole and the surrounding area, the Arctic is an ice-covered region that is frozen for much of the year.

Cold water survivors
Animals living in the Arctic are adapted to the extreme cold. Seals, sealions and walruses have a thick layer of fat, or blubber, just beneath their skin. This acts like an insulating blanket, keeping them warm.

Beneath the ice
In the summer, the numbers of plankton in the water explodes. These tiny living things are food for many animals, from fish to whales. The yearly abundance of fish attracts long-toothed narwhals and Greenland sharks.

Ice hunters

Polar bears are the world's largest land carnivores. They live on land and breathe air, but they can also swim over 100 km without stopping. When hunting for seals, they lie low on pack ice and wait for seals to pop up through breathing holes before snatching them.

Shrinking ice

Global warming has disastrous consequences for the Arctic. The melting pack ice forces polar bears to hunt over smaller areas, even walking into human towns and settlements in search of food.

Arctic summer ice has shrunk by

34%

since 1979.

ONE RECENT STUDY PREDICTS THAT SHIPS WILL BE ABLE TO SAIL THROUGH OPEN WATER RIGHT UP TO THE NORTH POLE BY 2040.

Southern Ocean
OCEAN FOOD CHAIN

Surrounding the Antarctic, the Southern Ocean is the windiest and coldest ocean on the planet. Despite its extreme conditions, the ocean blooms into life every summer.

Tiny treats
As summer approaches and sea ice melts, tiny micro-organisms, called phytoplankton, flourish. These become food for larger zooplankton, such as krill. Together, these tiny living things are food for fish, seabirds and even whales.

Big eaters
Fish living in the Southern Ocean include eelpouts and snailfish, but the truly big eaters are the baleen whales that migrate to the region to feed on krill. Among these are the biggest animals on Earth – blue whales. A blue whale can eat more than 3,500 kg of krill in one day!

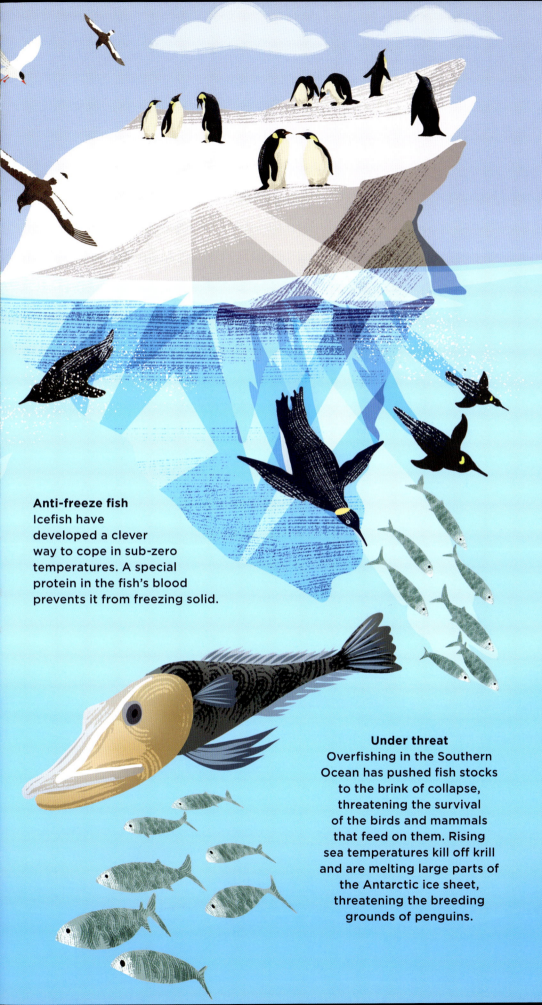

Anti-freeze fish
Icefish have developed a clever way to cope in sub-zero temperatures. A special protein in the fish's blood prevents it from freezing solid.

Under threat
Overfishing in the Southern Ocean has pushed fish stocks to the brink of collapse, threatening the survival of the birds and mammals that feed on them. Rising sea temperatures kill off krill and are melting large parts of the Antarctic ice sheet, threatening the breeding grounds of penguins.

Glossary

Carnivore an animal that eats meat

Climate change changes in Earth's climate, including the rising temperatures of global warming

Delta a triangular area formed when a river splits into several branches before it enters the sea

Dynamite fishing the use of explosives in fishing to stun or kill fish

Ecosystem a community of plants and animals that live and interact within a habitat

Endangered a species that is at risk of extinction due to environmental changes or human behaviour

Equator an imaginary line that runs around the middle of Earth, dividing it into northern and southern hemispheres

Food chain a sequence that shows how species rely on each other for food, with smaller plants and animals being eaten by larger animals

Indigenous originating from a particular place or country

Invertebrates a type of animal that does not have a spine

Marrow soft, spongy tissue that exists inside bones

Microbes tiny living things that include many types of bacteria, fungi and algae

Migration the seasonal movement of animals from one region to another, often to feed or breed

Minerals natural substances found in Earth's rocks, sand and soil

Molten when a material is so hot it has melted into its liquid form

Nutrients substances that are important for living things to survive

FURTHER INFORMATION

WEBSITES
www.natgeokids.com
www.nasa.gov/kidsclub
www.oceanservice.noaa.gov/kids/

MUSEUMS

Science Museum
Exhibition Road, South Kensington, London SW7 2DD

Oxford University Museum of Natural History
Parks Rd, Oxford, OX1 3PW

Photosynthesis the process in which green plants make food out of sunlight, carbon dioxide and water

Pollution waste substances and materials, like plastic, that contaminate the natural environment

Predator an animal that hunts other living things (prey)

Pressure a way of measuring the amount of force exerted on something

Prey an animal that is hunted by another for food

Protein a substance found in food that helps living things grow

Sediment tiny pieces of solid material, like rocks and soil

Storm surge sea levels that are unusually high as a result of a storm

Tropical the regions of the world that lie on either side of the equator

BOOKS

The Oceans Explored series by Claudia Martin (Wayland, 2021).
This series studies all aspects of the world's oceans, including the different habitats, species and the threats faced.

Infomojis: Ocean Life by Jon Richards and Ed Simkins (Wayland, 2018).
Discover incredible facts about the oceans with graphics, diagrams and custom-made 'infomojis'.

Index

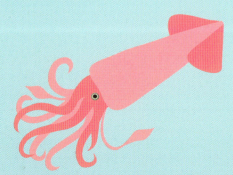
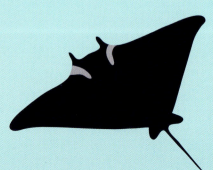